BEARS

Polar Bears

Stuart A. Kallen
ABDO & Daughters

visit us at
www.abdopub.com

Published by Abdo & Daughters, 4940 Viking Drive, Suite 622, Edina, Minnesota 55435.

Copyright © 1998 by Abdo Consulting Group, Inc., Pentagon Tower, P.O. Box 36036, Minneapolis, Minnesota 55435 USA. International copyrights reserved in all countries. No part of this book may be reproduced in any form without written permission from the publisher.

Printed in the United States.

Cover Photo credits: Peter Arnold, Inc.
Interior Photo credits: Peter Arnold, Inc.

Edited by Lori Kinstad Pupeza

Library of Congress Cataloging-in-Publication Data

Kallen, Stuart A., 1955-
      Polar Bears / Stuart A. Kallen
      p.   cm. -- (Bears)
      Includes index.
      Summary: Briefly describes the physical characteristics, habitat, and behavior of polar bears.
      ISBN 1-56239-593-9
      1. Polar bear--juvenile literature. [1. Polar bear. 2. Bears.]
      I. Title. II. Series: Kallen, Stuart A., 1955- Bears.
      QL737.C27K346   1998
      599.74'446--dc20   95-52341
                                       CIP
                                       AC

Contents

Polar Bears and Their Family

Polar bears are **mammals**. Like humans, they breathe air with lungs, are **warm blooded**, and **nurse** their young with milk.

Bears first **evolved** around 40 million years ago. They were small, meat-eating, tree-climbing animals. The early bears were related to coyotes, wolves, foxes, raccoons, and even dogs. Today, there are eight different **species** of bear. They live in 50 countries on 3 **continents**.

The Inuits call polar bears "Nanook." These white bears live in a land of endless ice and snow. Their scientific name, *Ursus maritimus* means "sea bear." Polar bears are usually found swimming the sea in search of food. Today there are about 20,000 to 40,000 polar bears worldwide.

Polar bears during the fall.

Size, Shape, and Color

Polar bears are some of the largest bears in the world. Females grow until they are 4 years old and weigh about 660 pounds (300 kg). Males grow until they are 8 years old and weigh about 1,200 pounds (545 kg). Males can grow from 8.25 to 11.5 feet (2.5 to 3.5 m) from nose to tail. The largest polar bear ever found was 12 feet (3.6 m) long and weighed 2,210 pounds (1,002 kg).

The polar bear has a stocky body. It has a longer neck and smaller head than most other bears. The polar bear has huge front paws. The back paws are larger and are webbed for swimming. The bear has a small stub of a tail and small, furry ears. The bear's lips and nose are black.

The coat of a polar bear is white with some yellow. Each hair is clear and hollow. The hollow hairs trap the warmth of the sun and deliver it to

the bear's skin. The hollow hair also helps the polar
bear float in water. The bear has 2 to 4 inches (5 to
10 cm) of blubbery fat under the fur. This also
keeps the bear warm and helps it to swim.

A polar bear walking.

Where They Live

Polar bears live in the North Pole, in the countries of Canada, Greenland, Norway, Russia, and the American state of Alaska. The Arctic Ocean surrounds the North Pole ice cap and is frozen all the time. But the edges melt where the sea meets land. The ice breaks during the summer every year. This is where the polar bear is at home.

Polar bears hunt in the sea and live in areas where open sea mixes with ice shelves. Polar bears can swim for 60 miles without resting. The big white bears ride ice flows for hundreds of miles.

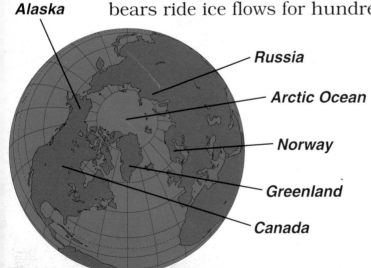

Alaska

Russia

Arctic Ocean

Norway

Greenland

Canada

Polar bears are also great walkers. They travel huge distances every year. Even though they walk slowly—2.5 miles per hour (4 kmph)—they may roam across 100,000 square miles (259,000 sq km) in a lifetime.

A polar bear on the frozen landscape.

Senses

Polar bears have excellent eyesight and hearing. Their noses are so sensitive that they can smell a seal over 20 miles (32 km) away. Scientists have watched polar bears march in a straight line for 40 miles (64 km) to catch an animal they sniffed in the wind. Polar bears can also sniff out seal **dens** that are covered by ice and snow three feet (one meter) deep.

Polar bears will cover their black noses with snow or ice so that other animals cannot see them as well. One scientist saw a polar bear move a large chunk of ice onto a bear trap. The ice sprang the trap and the bear ate the bait in the middle.

Opposite page: Polar bears have black noses.

Defense

Polar bears are very strong. They move giant chunks of ice with one paw. No animal of equal size is as powerful as a polar bear. A polar bear may kill a seal with a single blow to the neck.

Sometimes polar bears will fight with walruses. Both animals eat seals. The walrus is the only animal the polar bear fears. Human hunters are the main threat to polar bears.

Polar bears are careful of anything that comes near them. Polar bears attack for two reasons—to get food and to defend themselves. A polar bear can easily run 25 mph (40 kmph) for short distances.

Opposite page: Two polar bears playfighting.

Food

Seals are the main food for polar bears. Other bears eat roots, berries, and vegetable matter, but not the polar bear. Polar bears eat seals, walruses, fish, and crabs. If a dead whale washes on shore, polar bears will eat that too.

When out on the ice, a polar bear may go for weeks with no food. The bear lives off its stored fat. Polar bears have huge stomachs that can hold 150 pounds (70 kg) of food. To stay healthy, a polar bear must eat a seal every five or six days.

When bears hunt seals, they wait by the seal's breathing hole in the ice. A bear will wait there without moving for up to 14 hours. When the seal sticks his nose through the hole, the bear springs forward. It grabs the seal's head in its powerful jaws and kills it. With incredible strength, the bear will stand up pulling the 250 pound (113 kg) seal through the ice.

A polar bear searching for food in Canada.

Bear Hibernation

Polar bears dig winter shelters to escape very bad weather. Females stay in the shelters to have babies. This behavior is a mild form of **hibernation**, called "denning."

Denning usually begins by mid-October or early November. The **dens** are dug into snowbanks on south-facing slopes, to get the most warmth from the sun. The largest den may be three feet (one meter) high, and ten feet (three meters) long. The chambers are oval rooms with a tunnel leading into them. The body heat of the bear may raise the temperature inside the den to 40° F (4.4° C).

Females will have **cubs** inside the den. Males will wander throughout the winter and sleep for long periods. This is called "walking hibernation."

A polar bear in a snow den.

Babies

Female polar bears will begin to breed for the first time when they are five or six years old.

Pregnant females get very fat before denning. They enter their **dens** in October and give birth to **cubs** in January. The cubs are blind and helpless. They weigh only 20 ounces (.6 kg) each. The cubs remain in the den until late March or April. They grow quickly on their mother's fatty milk.

By spring the cubs may weigh between 22 and 33 pounds (10 to 15 kg). They leave the den and sit at the entrance for a few weeks. At the slightest sign of danger, the cubs run back into the den.

When they are large enough, the cubs begin to wander with their mother across the frozen tundra. She hunts for seals and teaches her cubs to do the same. When the mother goes into the water, the cubs cling to her back and ride her piggyback.

By August the **cubs** weigh 100 pounds (45 kg). They stay in the **den** with the mother for one or two more winters. Sometimes the cubs will live with the mother for four years.

Polar bear mother and cubs rest together on the snow.

Polar Bear Facts

Scientific Name: *Ursus maritimus* - the "sea bear"

Average Size: 660 pounds (300 kg). Males weigh from 1,100 to 1,322 pounds (500 to 600 kg). Males measure between 8.25 and 11.5 feet (2.5 to 3.5 m) from nose to tail. The largest polar bear ever found was 12 feet (3.6 m) long and weighed 2,210 pounds (1,002 kg).

Where They're Found: Norway, Greenland, Canada, Russian Siberia, and the American state of Alaska.

Opposite page: A Polar bear in Hudson Bay, Canada.

Glossary

Arctic Circle - the very cold region near the North Pole.

continent (KAHN-tih-nent) - one of the seven main land masses: Europe, Asia, Africa, North America, South America, Australia, and Antarctica.

cub - a baby bear.

den - a cave, hole in the ground, or hole in a tree used by a bear for a shelter.

evolve - for a species to develop or change over millions of years.

hibernate - to spend the winter in a deep sleep.

mammal - a class of animals, including humans, that have hair and feed their young milk.

nurse - to feed a young animal or child milk from the mother's breast.

prey - an animal hunted and captured for food.

species (SPEE-sees) - a group of related living things that have the same basic characteristics.

warm blooded - an animal whose body temperature remains the same and warmer than the outside air or temperature.

Index

Central Children's

MAR 2009